The Adventures of Donald the Knight

Fearfully & Wonderfully Made

Darnell Weathersby
Illustrated by: Martynas Marchiusm

No part of this publication may be reproduced, stored in a retrieval system or transmitted in any form or by any means, electronic, mechanical, photocopying, recording, or otherwise, without express written permission of the author.

The Adventures of Donald the Knight
Fearfully and Wonderfully Made

Darnell Weathersby
https://www.theleadonemovement.com/
hello@theleadonemovement.com

©Copyright 2022 All rights reserved

ISBN 978-1-943342-50-1

Published by:
Destined To Publish | www.DestinedToPublish.com
Flossmoor, Illinois • 773-783-2981

To my son

Winston,

I pray that you will always
walk confidently
knowing your worth
as a
Man of God.

Donald came through the front door of his home, full of emotions, as his day in school was bad, especially during recess!

Donald's book bag felt heavy, and his shoulders sunk extra low.

Inside, his mom was preparing a snack and waiting for him to get home, like she always did. With his head down and his eyes starting to fill with tears, he walked inside and dropped his bag near the front door.

Trying hard to fight back the tears, he stood there and asked in a soft whisper, "Mom? Mom! Are you home? Where are you?"

His mom was just about to take a seat at the kitchen table to drink her afternoon tea.

She heard the defeated tone in Donald's voice and gently replied, "I'm in the kitchen, sweetie."

Once in the kitchen, Donald saw his mom at the counter, cleaning up from making his snack.

She comforted him with a gentle hug and invited him to take a seat next to her.

Donald slowly slumped down into the chair next to his mom.

He wanted to look into his mom's eyes but could no longer stop himself from crying.

As the tears ran down his face, he took a deep breath and asked, "When am I going to start getting some muscles, Mom?"

"At recess, some of my friends and I were having a contest for who could do the most pull-ups."

"When it was my turn, I didn't do good at all.

"My arms were burning and shaking. When I let go of the bar, I fell and hurt my ankle.

"All of my friends laughed at me and called me skinny. They pointed at my arms and legs."

Donald's mom calmly listened, concerned yet so proud of the big boy he was becoming.

She tried her best not to smile and hurt his feelings even more.

"Take a moment and dry your eyes. Look at me closely. Donald, it may be hard to believe right now,

"but your body is developing at just the right speed."

"I understand that many of your friends are growing faster than you. But it would not be fun to always compare yourself to how others look," she said.

She paused and reached out to hold his hand. With a look of compassion, she asked, "Do you remember the Sunday school lesson from last week?"

Donald instantly knew the lesson she was talking about. He closed his eyes. He could still see the image of his Sunday school teacher writing on the board, with her bible open in her hand.

Donald then replied,
"Yes, I do, mom.
It was from Psalm 139."

"What was the big lesson son?" asked his mom as she looked deep into his eyes.

"I am fearfully and wonderfully made," answered Donald half-heartedly with his shoulders slumped over.

"I can't hear you," said his mom.

Donald sat, nice and tall, grinning from ear to ear. He proclaimed, "God doesn't make any junk, so I am fearfully and wonderfully made!"

"I praise You,
for I am Fearfully and Wonderfully made.

Marvelous are Your work, and I know this very well."

Donald's mom then asked, "What does it mean to be fearless at school, son?"

Donald paused for a moment to really think about her question.

He then answered,
"It's like I have a super power!

"God helps me to be strong when I feel weak. He helps me to be kind when others are being mean to me. It's an honor to be different, like the knights in the movies.

"I could be known as **Donald the Knight**"

At that moment, Donald's mom was standing tall next to him.

"I like the sound of that— **Donald the Knight**

Donald, promise me that you will never forget that."

His mom gave him one of her famous hugs.

Then she whispered into his ear, "There will be days that you don't feel special, but just remember that you are God's masterpiece.

You are a work in progress, so sit back and enjoy the journey."

Parent Reflection

1. What are some areas in which your child lacks confidence in this season of life?

2. What are some of the vessels being used to deliver negative messages to your child?

3. What are some ways in which you can proactively protect your child from these negative messages?

4. What are some positive messages with which you can intentionally replace those negative messages?

5. Rate your current level of communication with your child from 1–5, with 5 being that you connect daily to share and reflect on how the day has gone and 1 being that your child is consistently left to interpret life on their own.

Child Reflection

1. What are some areas in which you lack confidence right now?

2. What are some of the negative messages that you are being told?

3. How can your parents and friends help you think more positively about yourself?

4. Rate the quality time you spend with your parents 1–5, with 5 being that they are available to talk every day and 1 being that they are rarely available and always busy.

5. How can your parents make more time for you? At what time of the day would you enjoy connecting the most? Why?

Darnell Weathersby, M.Ed.

Having served as an educator for over 19 years, Darnell is exposed daily to the harsh reality that we live in a fallen world. The impact of sin upon our children grows with each passing generation. Unfortunately, it seems that the core values of the Christian faith that we attempt to instill in our children are being challenged increasingly earlier.

The underlying theme of this book series provides parents with a unique resource to refer to as they instruct their children on how to successfully navigate the potential pitfalls of peer pressure and low self-esteem.

Darnell is a graduate of Trinity International University with a BA in Elementary Education and Temple University with a Masters in Educational Leadership. He has assumed the roles of teacher, Assistant Principal and Acting Principal in both urban and suburban school districts across the country. Darnell currently serves as a high school Administrator. He is the proud husband of 17 years to Sharnell and father to their two children.

Made in the USA
Monee, IL
09 December 2022

20410850R00024